WHO? WHAT? WHY?

WHAT IS
TERRORISM?

ANNABEL SAVERY

WAYLAND
www.waylandbooks.co.uk

First published in Great Britain in 2017 by Wayland

Copyright © Hodder and Stoughton Limited, 2017

ISBN 978 1 5263 0689 0
10 9 8 7 6 5 4 3 2 1

Wayland
An imprint of
Hachette Children's Group
Part of Hodder & Stoughton
Carmelite House
50 Victoria Embankment
London EC4Y ODZ

An Hachette UK Company
www.hachette.co.uk
www.hachettechildrens.co.uk

A catalogue for this title is available from the British Library.

Printed in China.

MIX
Paper from
responsible sources
FSC® C104740

Produced for Wayland
by White-Thomson Publishing Ltd
www.wtpub.co.uk
Editor: Annabel Savery
Designer: Dan Prescott, Couper Street Type Co.
Consultant: Philip Parker

Picture acknowledgements:
(c = centre, r = right, l = left, t = top, b = bottom)
Getty Images: 12 GERY Gerard / Contributor, 15 William L. Rukeyser / Contributor, 17b CHOO YOUN-
KONG / Staff, 18 AHMAD AL-RUBAYE / Staff, 20 Bettmann / Contributor, 22c Alain MINGAM /
Contributor, 23b Pool / Pool, 24 Anadolu Agency / Contributor, 26 ODD ANDERSEN / Staff, 29 Michael
Ochs Archives / Stringer, 31 Peter Charlesworth / Contributor, 33 AFP / Stringer, 36 Anadolu Agency /
Contributor, 43 NIKLAS HALLE'N / Stringer; istock by Getty Images: 21 Allkindza, 22b evgovorov, 10
TonyBaggett; Shutterstock: Cover Prometheus72, 1 & 6 Asianet-Pakistan, 3 & 19 Frederic Legrand –
COMEO, 4 lonndubh, 8–9 Joseph Sohm, 8 cr Dan Howell, 9 t Anthony Correia, 13 Alessia Pierdomenico,
14 Frontpage, 16 EAZN, 23c Ed-Ni Photo, 25 Veselin Borishev, 27 Monkey Business Images, 28 Rena Schild,
30 Alberto Loyo, 32 Melanie Lemahieu, 34 Eugenio Marongiu, 35 pixinoo, 37b JStone, 38 Prometheus72, 39
tornadoflight, 40 Nicescene, 41c Sheila Fitzgerald, 42 Elena Dijour, 44 veronicka, 45 James Kennedy NI;
WIKI COMMONS: 11t Welcome Images, 11b Library of Congress.

All graphic elements courtesy of Shutterstock.

Infographics sources: Bureau of Counterterrorism and Countering Violent Extremism, Country Reports
on Terrorism 2015: 41 b; Global Terrorism Index, 2016, Institute for Economics and Peace: 5, 7, 37t; Pew
Research Centre 2017 19.

Every attempt has been made to clear copyright. Should there be any inadvertent omission please apply to the
publisher for rectification.

CONTENTS

WHY DO WE NEED TO TALK ABOUT TERRORISM?

On Monday 22 May 2017, as people left a music concert given by Ariana Grande, a man walked into the foyer of the Manchester Arena and detonated a homemade bomb. The blast killed twenty-two people and injured 116 more. As news of the Manchester Arena terrorist attack spread, people in shock and horror asked themselves: who would do such a thing and why?

TALKING ABOUT TERRORISM

Terrorism is an incredibly difficult thing to understand, and can be hard to talk about. Events that we hear and read about can be upsetting, frightening and confusing. However, we can try to understand the reasons why people commit terrorist actions, and what threat they pose to our society.

AN OLD PROBLEM

Terrorism is not a new problem. People have used this form of attack throughout history to bring about political change or to draw attention to a cause. In recent times, it can seem as though terrorism is being used more than ever before. This is partly because of the availability of information, but also because attacks are happening in more countries, rather than just in those where there is existing conflict, such as civil war.

Flowers and tributes are left in memory of the victims of the Manchester attack. ⬇

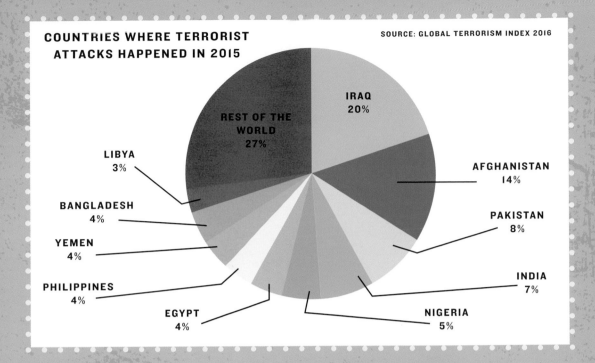

COUNTRIES WHERE TERRORIST ATTACKS HAPPENED IN 2015

SOURCE: GLOBAL TERRORISM INDEX 2016

- IRAQ 20%
- AFGHANISTAN 14%
- PAKISTAN 8%
- INDIA 7%
- NIGERIA 5%
- EGYPT 4%
- PHILIPPINES 4%
- YEMEN 4%
- BANGLADESH 4%
- LIBYA 3%
- REST OF THE WORLD 27%

A RELATIVE THREAT

In August 2017, two attacks in Barcelona and Cambrils, Spain left 13 dead and 100 injured. Although attacks such as these are frightening, it is important to remember that the reason they dominate the media is because they are rare. In the west, people are more likely to be hurt or killed in traffic accidents than they are by terrorism. In 2015, seventy per cent of deaths caused by terrorism happened in just five countries: Afghanistan, Iraq, Nigeria, Pakistan and Syria.

THE MEDIA

The term 'media' includes all forms of mass communication: radio, television, newspapers and digital channels. The world today is buzzing with information. When an event happens, phones beep, screens flash and the press gather. Alongside mainstream news sources are other sources of information such as social media and comment pages. It is important to look at the source of what you are reading. While news reports are mainly factual, other comment-based reports or discussion threads will include opinion and hearsay, which often distort the facts.

WHAT IS TERRORISM?

Terrorism is the use of violence to terrify people. It is constructed from the word 'terror', meaning 'extreme fear'. A terrorist is someone who wants to create a feeling of extreme fear in others, hoping that this fear will cause people to behave in a certain way.

TYPES OF TERRORISM

Terrorism can be broadly split into types, but the boundaries of these definitions can be blurry.

Revolutionary terrorism is action taken by those who want to bring about a revolution. Nationalistic terrorism is action taken by groups who want to bring about independence for a nation that is ruled by another. Religious terrorism is action taken for reasons of religion. Today, religious terrorism is committed by those who follow extreme branches of some religions, such as Islamic extremists, or Islamists. While these groups claim to be acting in defence of their faith, others see their actions as aggressive and inflammatory.

ACTS OF TERRORISM

Terrorism can take many forms. Actions are violent and often planned to cause as much harm as possible. Terrorists have used hijacks, kidnapping and the taking of hostages, with some hostages being subjected to torture. Bombs, weapons and vehicles have all been used to attack people. Terrorists are also starting to use the internet in actions known as cyberterrorism. Terrorism can be funded by the trade and trafficking of illegal drugs. This, as well as the violence used by drug traffickers, is known as narco-terrorism.

JUNE 2014 In 2014, Taliban fighters armed with grenades and guns attacked Karachi airport in Pakistan. 28 people were killed including 18 Taliban.

THE DIFFICULTY OF DEFINITIONS

Each country has a definition of terrorism, and these differ depending on the government and events in each country. These definitions are important because they are used by the police and security services to arrest and charge people with terrorist plots and offences.

> Terrorist groups use violence and threats of violence to publicise their causes and as a means to achieve their goals.
>
> . . . .
>
> **UK Security Service MI5**
>
> Terrorism includes the unlawful use of force and violence against persons or property to intimidate or coerce a government, the civilian population, or any segment thereof, in furtherance of political or social objectives.
>
> . . . . . .
>
> **US Code of Federal Regulations**

This map shows the impact of terrorism around the world. The darkest red colour indicates the countries most affected by terrorism.

Highest impact of terrorism

Lowest impact of terrorism
No impact of terrorism
Not included

7

SOURCE: GLOBAL TERRORISM INDEX 2016

WHAT IS THE 'WAR ON TERROR'?

On 11 September 2001, four passenger planes were hijacked in the USA. Two of the planes were deliberately crashed into New York's World Trade Center. A third was crashed into the Pentagon. The fourth crashed in a field in Pennsylvania. Almost 3,000 people were killed in the attacks.

KEY LOCATIONS

The Twin Towers were two iconic buildings in New York's World Trade Center, the city's financial centre. The Pentagon in Washington DC is the headquarters of the US Department of Defense. The fourth plane did not reach its intended target but crashed in a field. Reports later found that the plane may have been crashed by the hijackers to prevent the passengers and crew retaking control.

WHO WERE THE HIJACKERS?

There were nineteen hijackers. They were members of the Islamist group al-Qaeda. All had been living in the USA before the time of the attacks. Some of the hijackers had commercial flight training, which allowed them to reroute the planes once the hijackers had taken control.

When they were completed in 1985, the Twin Towers were the tallest buildings in the world and became an iconic feature of New York's skyline.

Following the attacks, the towers collapsed killing and injuring thousands of people.

Firefighters and emergency crew work at Ground Zero, the site of the Twin Towers after their collapse.

SEPT 2001

THE USA'S RESPONSE

President George W Bush's speech in the aftermath of the attacks made it clear that the USA would seek out not only the organisers of the attack but anyone who supported or protected them. Al-Qaeda's principal base was in Afghanistan, a country largely ruled by the Taliban, who supported al-Qaeda's Islamist views. Attacks were launched by the USA and allied forces on Afghanistan and many supporters of the groups were killed or captured. President Bush used the phrase 'war on terror' in a speech following the September 2001 attacks. It has become symbolic of the USA's strategy to prevent further terrorist action.

> "
> Our war on terror begins with al-Qaeda, but it does not end there. It will not end until every terrorist group of global reach has been found, stopped and defeated.
>
> • • • • • •
>
> **President Bush,
> State of the Union address,
> 21 September 2001**
> "

WHEN DID TERRORISM START?

Terrorism has no exact starting point, but below are some historical examples of terror as we recognise it today – people using violence to create fear, with the aim of bringing about or resisting change.

ASSASSINS

Although the term has a different meaning today, 'the Assassins' was originally used for a group of people in the eleventh century. They were a Persian religious sect called the Nizari Ismailis. Without their own army, the Nizari used individuals to spy on and assassinate key figures within the ruling powers they opposed. The assassinations were carried out by only a few people.

THE GUNPOWDER PLOT

In 1605, a group of English Roman Catholics plotted to blow up Parliament and kill the Protestant king, his wife and son. They hoped to replace them with a ruler who would be more favourable to English Roman Catholics. The group concealed barrels of gunpowder under the Parliament buildings, ready for a meeting on 5 November. The plot was uncovered and one conspirator, Guy Fawkes, was discovered. Under torture, Fawkes gave the names of the others in the group. Four were killed resisting arrest, the others were tried and executed.

ASSASSINS IN LEGEND

The first tales of the mysterious assassins came to Europe with travellers. They told of a murderous group who lived in the mountains and were ruled by a mysterious leader, the Old Man of the Mountain.

There was a little truth in these legends but it has been twisted through hearsay and rumour. Many tales were told by people who were hostile to the Nizari.

Rather than their actions granting more rights to the Roman Catholics, the Gunpowder Plot led to more suspicion of Catholics and harsher laws against them.

THE SPANISH INQUISITION

In 1478, the Pope gave permission for Catholic monarchs to appoint inquisitors. They were to investigate those practising religions other than Catholicism, but their powers quickly grew. Torture and confiscation were both used to frighten and intimidate. The Inquisition resulted in some 160,000 Jews and 300,000 Muslims being expelled from Spain by 1614.

The inside of a jail of the Spanish Inquisition

LE GRAND TERREUR

The Great Terror took place during the French Revolution. As war raged, France was declared a Republic. In 1793, the Revolutionary government decided to impose an order of 'terror', meaning that they would take harsh measures against anyone suspected of acting against the Revolution. At least 300,000 were arrested, 17,000 were executed, and it is thought that another 10,000 died in prison.

THE KU KLUX KLAN

This was a white supremacist movement that began in 1866 in Tennessee, USA. It was formed from those who opposed racial equality. They used violence, including whipping, to intimidate the black population, who were newly freed from slavery, and their white supporters.

The Ku Klux Klan wore white robes and pointed hoods, clothes designed to frighten people.

WHAT ARE THE TYPES OF TERRORISM?

As we have seen, terrorism can be broadly split into three types: revolutionary, nationalistic and religious. However, while some individuals or groups may operate for one single reason, others may act for a combination of all three reasons.

REVOLUTIONARY TERRORISM

Revolutionary terrorism is action taken by those who want to bring about a revolution. They act in the hope that the ruling power in a country will be overthrown in favour of a new system. One such example is the Italian Red Brigades or *Brigate Rosse*. They operated in Italy in the 1970s with the aim of demonstrating that the ruling government was weak, so that like-minded people would rise up, and force them out of power.

The *Brigate Rosse* were a militant organisation, which means that they were willing to use violence to achieve their aims. The group carried out more than 50 attacks and brought about almost 50 deaths through kidnapping and assassination, and firebombing factories and warehouses. It took over ten years, but by systematic police work involving the identification and arrest of group leaders and members, the group had largely been destroyed by the late 1980s.

In 1978, 46 members of the *Brigate Rosse* we put on trial in Italy. They were held in cages to prevent any attempt to free them.

MAR 1978

THE GOOD TERRORIST ...

There is a difficult argument about whether there can ever be such a thing as a good terrorist. Today it is hard to imagine, but in recent history there are those who have fought against regimes that were unjust, and who used terror themselves.

The Resistance were people who fought against Hitler's regime during the Second World War. Some of their actions were peaceful, such as publishing newspapers, helping Jews or helping foreign soldiers stranded in enemy territory. Other actions were violent, as they attacked German patrols or committed sabotage to try and weaken the German forces.

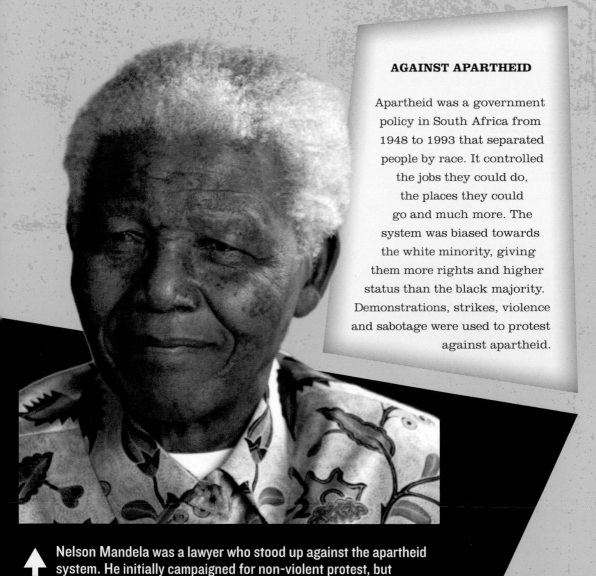

AGAINST APARTHEID

Apartheid was a government policy in South Africa from 1948 to 1993 that separated people by race. It controlled the jobs they could do, the places they could go and much more. The system was biased towards the white minority, giving them more rights and higher status than the black majority. Demonstrations, strikes, violence and sabotage were used to protest against apartheid.

Nelson Mandela was a lawyer who stood up against the apartheid system. He initially campaigned for non-violent protest, but after the Sharpeville massacre in 1960, began to support acts of terrorism against the government. He was arrested and spent 26 years in prison. He was released in 1990, and in 1994 became President of South Africa's first multi-ethnic government.

NATIONALISTIC TERRORISM

Nationalist organisations work either towards independence for one nation that is ruled by another, or for an independent state or country for a particular ethnic group. Some groups campaign peacefully, while others resort to terrorism and violence.

LIBERATION TIGERS OF TAMIL EELAM

The Liberation Tigers of Tamil Eelam (LTTE) insurgent group formed in Sri Lanka in 1976, with the aim of protetcting the rights of the minority Tamil population. They have become known as the Tamil Tigers. They wanted to create an independent Tamil state. Funded partly by bank robberies and drug smuggling, the Tamil Tigers were able to control territory on the Jaffna Peninsula.

The group conducted many terrorist attacks, including bombings and assassinations of key political figures including the Sri Lankan President, Ranasinghe Premadasa. Like other groups, the Tamil Tigers have made use of suicide bombers. This is when a person wears or carries a device close to them, killing themselves in the detonation. One of the worst attacks by the Tamil Tigers was a suicide bomb in the country's capital city Colombo, in which 100 people were killed.

Although a ceasefire was signed in 2002, violence continued and it was abandoned in 2008. Government troops were able to capture rebel strongholds and bring their actions to an end. However, thousands of civilians were killed during the violence.

On 20 February 2009, Tamils from across Europe held a demonstration against Sri Lanka's treatment of Tamil rebels.

THE IRISH REPUBLICAN ARMY

In 1921, a treaty separated the independent Republic of Ireland from Northern Ireland, which remained part of the United Kingdom. Since this time, there has always been a movement that supports Ireland and Northern Ireland being united and independent from the UK. Part of this movement was a militant organisation called the Irish Republican Army (IRA).

THE TROUBLES

The time between 1970 and 1998 is known as The Troubles because of the high level of unrest. On 30 January 1972, thirteen Catholic protesters were killed by British paratroopers leading to an escalation of violence. This day became known as Bloody Sunday. In 1974, IRA terrorists targeted a bus transporting British soldiers and their families, and bombed pubs in Guildford and Birmingham.

It is thought that 1,800 people were killed by Republican groups between 1969 and 1994. A ceasefire was announced in 1994 and peace talks began. It was a long, difficult process but in 1998, the Good Friday Agreement was signed and peace was established.

JAN 1972

Protesters face British paratroopers on Bloody Sunday.

RELIGIOUS TERRORISM

In the past, religious terrorism has come about when religious groups have been treated unfairly. However, today religious terrorism is largely caused by religious extremism – see pages 17–19. This makes it all the more important to remember that the vast majority of people of any faith practise it peacefully, and with tolerance of other religions.

> " Everyone has the right to freedom of thought, conscience and religion; this right includes freedom to change his religion or belief, and freedom, either alone or in community with others and in public or private, to manifest his religion or belief in teaching, practice, worship or observance.
>
> **Article 18 of the Universal Declaration of Human Rights adopted by the United Nations in 1948** "

RELIGIOUS BELIEFS

A religion is a set of ideas that people choose to believe in and live by. A religion's principles are often set out in ancient books that are believed to hold the words of the religion's god, as told to prophets on earth.

There are reported to be over 4,000 religions in the world and each has its own set of beliefs and laws that followers live by. The strength with which beliefs are held is different for each individual. Some people believe strongly, for others, it is part of their life, but they practise less actively. In most countries, people are free to practise any religion they choose. However, in some countries, people are treated unfairly or attacked for their religious beliefs.

Many religions are centred around ancient texts. Here, a Jewish boy and his teacher look at a Torah scroll in Israel.

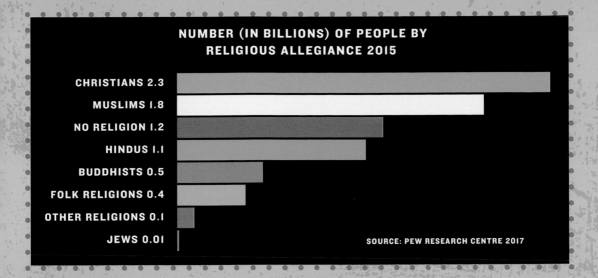

NUMBER (IN BILLIONS) OF PEOPLE BY RELIGIOUS ALLEGIANCE 2015

CHRISTIANS 2.3

MUSLIMS 1.8

NO RELIGION 1.2

HINDUS 1.1

BUDDHISTS 0.5

FOLK RELIGIONS 0.4

OTHER RELIGIONS 0.1

JEWS 0.01

SOURCE: PEW RESEARCH CENTRE 2017

EXTREMISM

Many of the world's religions have extreme, or fundamentalist, groups. Extremists live their lives by strictly following the words and laws set out in their religion's sacred text or book. These books were written at a time when language, life and society were very different. This means they can be interpreted in many ways, and different groups believe different readings.

⬆ Two Canadian tourists bring flowers to the scene of the Bali bomb attack in 2002.

BALI BOMBINGS

In October 2002, two bombs exploded on the Indonesian island of Bali and 202 people were killed. The first was a suicide bomb that was detonated inside a bar, the second was a larger car bomb that was detonated as those in the bar were evacuated into the street.

Islamist group Jemaah Islamiyah were identified as responsible for the attacks. They formed in the 1980s with the intention of spreading fundamentalist Islam in Indonesia. Since the 1990s, they have been linked to al-Qaeda, an international Islamist organisation.

RELIGIOUS EXTREMISM AND ISLAM

Islam is the faith practised by Muslims. Within Islam, there are two main branches – Sunni and Shia. There are those who practise an extreme form of Islam who have become known today as Islamists, Islamic fundamentalists or Islamist extremists. They are intolerant of those who practise other religions, or who are without faith.

SHARIA

Sharia is the word for Islamic law. These laws come from the Qur'an and from the Hadith. They apply to all aspects of a Muslim person's life, from prayer and marriage, to food and dress. For Islamist groups, the words of old texts are taken literally, and not read with today's world and society in mind. Islamists see it as their duty to enforce these laws.

JIHAD

Jihad and jihadi are terms that are used frequently in the media. Jihad is often said to mean 'holy war' but its real meaning is more complicated. Literally, 'jihad' means 'struggle'. In one sense, this means that it can be challenging to live as a faithful Muslim. In another sense, it means the struggle to defend Islam and protect Muslims from being attacked for their faith.

Boys walk through the city of Mosul, Iraq, following fighting between government forces and so-called jihadis from the Islamic State group.

RADICALISATION

When a person is radicalised, they are persuaded to take on extreme views. In the case of Islamist radicalisation, people are convinced that to live a 'good' Muslim life, they must follow Islamists' strict interpretation of sharia law and impose it on others. They may be persuaded to become jihadis and take up an armed struggle against anyone thought to threaten Islam.

ISLAMIC STATE

Islamic State, or IS, is a group of militant Islamists who have grown in strength since 2014. They are also known as ISIS and ISIL. Several smaller extremist groups joined with elements of the larger terrorist group to form Islamic State. They support the use of violence and see people who do not support their version of Islam as enemies who threaten their faith.

IS claim to follow the Sunni branch of Islam. Their goal is to create an all-Muslim state known as a caliphate, under a leader called a caliph. Led by a man called Abu Bakr al-Baghdadi, the group managed to gain territory in Iraq and Syria. Their propaganda asks people to join the state and give loyalty to the leader. IS use the internet and social media to target young people and persuade them to join the group. By 2016, IS was known to be active in 28 countries.

NOV 2015 Candles are lit for the victims of multiple attacks in Paris on 13 November 2015. 130 died in the attacks that are thought to have been planned by Islamic State.

HOW HAS TERRORISM CHANGED?

In 1970, three planes were hijacked mid-flight by militants from a group called the Popular Front for the Liberation of Palestine (PFLP). The planes were flown to Jordan. Some passengers were allowed to leave the planes, but 56 were moved to a secret location. They were held hostage until the hijackers' demands were met and seven Palestinian dissidents were released from prison.

CHANGING TERRORISM

The example of the PFLP hostage taking shows how terrorism began to change in the twentieth century. Before this, attacks had principally been aimed at military or political targets. However, with the use of both hijacking and hostage-taking, civilians had begun to be targets for terrorism.

In taking hostages, terrorists want to force governments to accept their demands, in order to protect innocent citizens.

Along with targeting civilians, there has been a rise in the use of suicide bombings. This tactic allows terrorists to get close to their target, without the use of advanced military technology.

 Just minutes after the last hostages were allowed to leave, the PFLP blew up the hijacked planes.

INTERNATIONAL TERRORISM

As groups such as the PFLP show, terrorism has become increasingly international. With advances in travel technology, people can move easily between countries and across borders. Today, terrorism is motivated by causes that are not only within specific countries. The group al-Qaeda was based largely in Afghanistan but because they operate for religious reasons, they have a network that stretches all over the world.

AL-QAEDA

Al-Qaeda began operating in the 1980s, led by Osama bin Laden. They are an Islamist organisation responsible for some of the worst terrorist attacks in recent times, including the 9/11 attacks on the USA. The group is a vast international network and has established training camps in many countries.

Al-Qaeda's goal is to force the USA and other Western nations out of the Middle East. They also claim to be acting in revenge for wrongs they believe have been committed against Muslims over many centuries.

CYBERTERRORISM

Advances in computer technology have allowed everyone to have the digital world at their fingertips at any time. But this accessibility can also be used for disruptive or destructive purposes. Computer hacking is a form of crime where criminals break into secure networks to commit identity theft and fraud. Terrorists can make use of the advances in the digital world to commit crime, to raise funds, and to expand their communications network and influence.

Newspapers report the death of Osama bin Laden in September 2012. The al-Qaeda leader was found in hiding and killed by US forces, acting on the President's orders.

WHO USES TERRORISM?

Terrorism has been used by organisations, by governments and by individuals. In each case, the choice has been made to act with violence, rather than looking for a peaceful solution.

ORGANISATIONS THAT USE TERRORISM

Organisations form when people share an idea or problem, and discuss ideas for change. As these groups gain followers, they can become more active in trying to bring about change. Actions may begin with peaceful campaigning; however, some then turn to more violent means if their goals are not achieved.

In 1968, German students formed a protest movement against the way West Germany was being governed. A couple of students wanted to use radical methods and formed the Red Army Faction. They committed terrorist acts such as arson, bombing, kidnapping and assassination. The group extended its reach beyond West Germany, but lost support because of its violent actions.

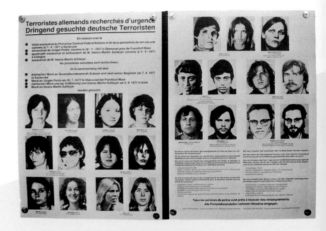

 1977: A French wanted poster for members of the Red Army Faction, also known as the Baader-Meinhof Group after the names of their leaders.

STATE TERRORISM

Terrorism has been used by governments against other governments, groups or even their own citizens. In the 1930s the Soviet Union was ruled by a dictator, Joseph Stalin. He ordered 'purges' where anyone suspected of disloyalty was either executed or sent to prison camps. The 'Great Purge' began with political figures and spread to ordinary citizens. Today, it can be difficult to prove that such state-directed terrorism is happening as authorities can support violence, without their connection to it being known.

Joseph Stalin became dictator of the Soviet Union in the late 1920s.

MILITARY DICTATORSHIPS

When a country is ruled by a dictator, that person has complete power. They have often come to power through an army taking control. This happened in Argentina in 1976. A military force took power under Lieutenant General Jorge Rafael Videla. He enforced a system of terror, also known as the 'Dirty War'. Those thought to oppose the government were kidnapped, captured, tortured and executed. The death toll is thought to be between 10,000 and 30,000. Many people simply disappeared – they were arrested by the authorities and never heard from again.

In 2008, mothers of some of those who disappeared during Argentinia's 'Dirty War' hold a demonstration asking for justice.

SADDAM HUSSEIN

Saddam Hussein became President of Iraq in 1979. He used a secret police network to suppress his opposition. He ordered the invasion of Iran and Kuwait, and his forces crushed internal rebellions. Many were killed in the violence and others fled as refugees.

US and allied forces took action against him in 1998 and 2003. Saddam fled but was later arrested. In 2005 he was put on trial and found guilty of crimes including illegal imprisonment, torture and killing.

Saddam Hussein stands to be sentenced in 2005.

ACTING ALONE

Many terrorist attacks, such as shootings or suicide bombings, are carried out by individuals. In most cases, they are linked to organisations that train and support them. In some cases, however, individuals act alone. Even when a terrorist acts alone, there are organisations, such as IS, who claim responsibility for the attack. They hope to draw attention to their cause, and give the impression that they have a far-reaching influence.

People are still trying to understand the process of self-radicalisation, when a person becomes radicalised without having direct contact with people with extreme views. Today, this often happens with the use of the internet. It is easy for people to become confused by events that they see or hear about. They may come to believe that violence is acceptable.

AN ATTACK IN ORLANDO, USA

On 12 June 2016, a 29-year-old man opened fire in a nightclub in Orlando, Florida. There were more than 300 people inside the venue; 49 people were killed and many more injured. Shortly before the attack, the gunman had called the police and told them he was loyal to IS. Although he was known to the FBI – the US Intelligence Service – they could not find links between him and IS.

MAY 2017

A suicide bomber drove a truck packed with explosives into Kabul, Afghanistan in May 2017. At least 90 people were killed and 400 injured.

WOMEN IN TERROR

Although the majority of terrorists are male, female militants are also part of terrorist movements. Women made up approximately 30 per cent of the *Brigate Rosse*, and roughly ten per cent of Western recruits to IS are female. One of the most well-known female terrorist groups is the Chechen Black Widows. They form part of an Islamist group within Chechnya and are women who have lost male relatives and loved ones in wars that Russia has fought against Islamist rebels.

Women suffer at the hands of radical groups, such as Islamic State, who enforce strict laws including dress codes and sex segregation. However, women also form part of such groups, and help to inflict these strict rules on other women. They also play a part in recruiting other women to the group and training female terrorists.

Floral tributes are left in the shell of a school in Beslan, Russia. In 2004, militants including Chechen Black Widows stormed the building, taking 1000 hostages. 300 were killed in the siege that followed.

WHY DO PEOPLE BECOME TERRORISTS?

A combination of circumstances, personal history, family situation, external influences and many other factors can make people turn to terrorism. People can also be persuaded into terrorism, rather than turning to it independently.

WHAT MAKES PEOPLE ACT?

Acts of terrorism are committed by people completely convinced that their cause is justified. This may be a path people take independently, as they are certain that there is a wrong that needs to be put right. Other people may have undergone radicalisation, whether by a group or by themselves.

Some people may have experienced suffering, such as losing loved ones through living in a war-torn area. They may have been subjected to harsh treatment because of their faith or ethnicity. People, particularly the young, can often feel extreme anger at situations that seem unfair. This can lead to them being more open to taking extreme actions themselves.

In 2016, a stolen lorry was driven into a busy Christmas market in Berlin, Germany. It was a deliberate attack by a man belonging to a terrorist cell loyal to IS.

DEC 2016

VULNERABLE PEOPLE

Anyone can come under the influence of a person or idea, but some people may be more vulnerable to radicalisation than others. Those more at risk are likely to have suffered loss or bullying, or be living in poverty. These circumstances can make a person feel sad, lost, alone or scared.

People looking to recruit to terrorist networks may target vulnerable young people. Being welcomed into a network may bring a feeling of belonging and security. Being given a role that feels important can give them a sense of control and self-esteem.

↑ Schools and faith groups are working with young people to discuss difficult issues, and to support those who may be vulnerable.

PROTECTION FROM RADICALISATION

There are many organisations that are working to protect young people from becoming targets for radicalisation. Schools and clubs are increasingly asked to look for signs that a person may be falling under the influence of someone else. These signs are hard to spot but might include changes in behaviour, becoming more distant, and rejecting activities they previously enjoyed.

SOCIAL MEDIA AND RECRUITMENT

Radical Islamist groups have been known to use social media channels to try to spread their message. Young people may be targeted with extreme statements or exciting promises. They may be exposed to violent and distressing images, or be shown people seeming to live a glorious life as part of the group.

27

WHY DO PEOPLE USE TERRORISM?

Choosing terrorism over other forms of action – such as political protest – is difficult to understand. It may be that groups turn to violence if they feel they are not being listened to in other ways. It is also seen as effective by certain groups, because of the media attention it brings.

A DEMONSTRATION

Groups that resort to terrorism are often relatively small. They are vastly outnumbered by military forces, and by civilians who do not support them. These groups turn to terrorism because they do not have the strength or finances to fight a war against larger forces. They know that a single attack can still shock and hurt people.

Terrorist groups know that the actions taken by a government following a terrorist attack can move more people towards their cause. If a government cuts trade with or supply routes to a terrorist-controlled area, civilians will also suffer. Similarly, if a government takes military action, civilians may be caught in the violence. Both of these actions can make civilians decide to join the terrorist cause.

APR 2017 A demonstration in Washington, USA, against air strikes in Syria. Many civilians have been killed and injured in these air strikes.

MEDIA ATTENTION

People who use terrorism recognise the efficiency of today's media industry. They know that terrorist attacks are shocking, and therefore bring huge amounts of public attention. The media is used as part of their demonstration.

It is estimated that the average person in the USA watched eight hours of coverage on the day of the September 2001 attacks. The same day, the news network CNN received 162 million hits on their website, compared to their daily average of 14 million.

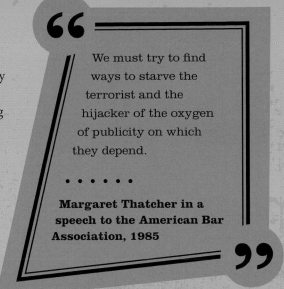

> We must try to find ways to starve the terrorist and the hijacker of the oxygen of publicity on which they depend.

Margaret Thatcher in a speech to the American Bar Association, 1985

MUNICH OLYMPICS 1972

In the summer of 1972, many televisions around the world were tuned to the Olympic Games in Munich. Eight terrorists from the Palestinian group Black September entered the athletes' rooms in the Olympic village and took nine Israeli athletes hostage. Then, they bargained with the German authorities for the release of 200 Palestinian prisoners held in Israel, as well as two Red Army Faction members. In the events that followed there was a rescue attempt that failed. All the hostages, five of their captors and a police man were killed. During the attack, Olympic organisers made the decision to keep broadcasting. Half a million people tuned in.

 Munich Olympics, 1972: Press cameramen take pictures as the police gather in front of the accommodation where the Israeli athletes are being held hostage.

29

WHAT DO TERRORISTS WANT?

The goals of terrorism can range from short term, such as the release of prisoners, to long-term, such as establishing a new state or overthrowing a government. For many atrocities committed today, it is hard for us to understand what the attacker hopes to achieve.

CHANGE AND REVOLUTION

Most terrorists are working for organisations that have larger goals. The group ETA is a militant organisation who want a separate, independent state for the Basque people of northern Spain and south-west France. ETA have carried out a number of violent attacks including kidnappings and bombings over their 40 years of activity, in which over 800 people have been killed. ETA announced in 2017 that they had completely disarmed, and peace talks are continuing.

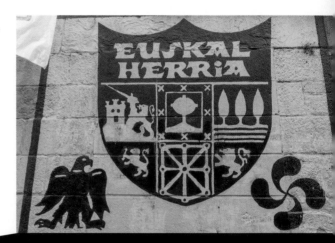

A mural showing the flag of the ETA movement. *Euskal Herria* means 'Basque nation'.

SETTING DEMANDS

In some cases, terrorists hold people in hostage situations and make demands for their safe return. Negotiations are difficult as the government and police must work to free the hostages, while trying not to give terrorists what they are demanding.

In 2013, Islamist militants linked to al-Qaeda took control of the In Amenas gas plant in Algeria. They held 800 employees hostage, including Algerian and international workers. They demanded the release of Islamist prisoners and the withdrawal of French military forces from Mali, a neighbouring country. Four days later, Algerian troops regained control of the site, but 40 workers and 29 militants were killed in the siege.

REMOVING MILITARY FORCES

In October 1983, a truck carrying explosives was driven
into a US Marine base in Beirut, Lebanon. In the explosion
that followed, 241 US service personnel were killed. In the
February following this event, US troops withdrew from
Lebanon. Later, it was believed that the group Hezbollah
carried out the attack. Hezbollah is a Shia Islamist group that
has been active in Lebanon since the 1980s. They have both
political and military operations.

It is thought that this event influenced Osama bin Laden's
plot to attack the USA in September 2001. He mistakenly
believed that the attacks would influence US and other
Western powers to leave any bases they had in the
Middle East and prevent them taking
action in the region.

Following the 1983 attack, US forces
and civilians – mainly diplomats and
aid workers and their families – are
evacuated from Beirut, Lebanon.

BRINGING FEAR

No matter what their eventual goal is, a terrorist's immediate aim is to cause fear. In the French Revolution, the system of terror used by the Revolutionary government (see page 11) was meant to frighten their opponents. For revolutionary and nationalist groups that threatened and kidnapped key political figures, the goal was to frighten other political figures from standing against them. Today, acts of terrorism are often used to reduce feelings of safety in ordinary civilians.

I'M AFRAID
BUT
I'M HERE

⬆ Paris 2016: Following a terrorist attack, a demonstrator shows that they want to stand against terrorism, despite the fear that violent action brings.

SHOWING WEAKNESS

Some terrorist attacks are designed to show weakness in a country's government. After an attack, people ask why, in a peaceful country, they can no longer feel secure. In this situation, terrorists hope to cause unrest as civilians become unhappy with their government. This may help revolutionary groups to overthrown one political system in favour of another.

MARTYRDOM

A martyr is someone who is killed for their religious beliefs. Some people connect religious motivations for terrorist attacks with the idea of martyrdom. Many of the larger world religions, such as Islam and Christianity, forbid suicide. However, some Islamist groups claim there are circumstances where it is acceptable, such as in war or jihad (see page 18) and so support suicide missions. They spread the message that such actions will lead to great rewards in the afterlife.

IS TERRORISM SUCCESSFUL?

Terrorism certainly brings about feelings of fear, and raises awareness of particular political or religious groups. However, fear is something that can be managed, and for the vast majority, the awareness that terrorism brings is negative. Politically, governments work constantly against terrorism and most will not negotiate with organisations until they renounce violence and look to find a peaceful route to a settlement.

LONDON 7/7

On the 7 July 2005, four suicide bombers attacked in London. They targeted busy transport – three underground trains and a bus – in the middle of the morning rush hour. 52 people were killed and hundreds more were injured.

Londoners refused to be intimidated by the attacks and continued to use public transport.

The bombers were British men with links to Islamist extremism. All four of them died in the attack, so could not be tried or questioned for their actions.

The wreckage of the bus that was targeted by a suicide bomber in July 2005.

WHAT ROLE DOES THE MEDIA PLAY?

The media runs throughout modern life and can feel inescapable. Traditionally, the role of the media is to communicate information to the world. Most countries have freedom of the press, meaning they are free to communicate the information they judge to be true and fair.

TERRORISM AND THE MEDIA

For the most part, advances in media technology are positive. News can spread within minutes and keeps us informed and up-to-date. However, these advances can also be used by those who wish to cause harm. Terrorists know that their actions will be front-page news and the more shocking they are, the faster news will spread.

When negative news stories focus on one particular ethnic or religious group, it can lead to misunderstandings. For example, media coverage of Islamist terrorists may give others the wrong idea that all Muslims have radical beliefs and lead to them being treated unfairly.

Muslims respond to the growing problem of Islamophobia, the dislike and unfair treatment of Muslims, that can result from the media's reports of Islamist terrorism.

I'M JUST MUSLIM NOT A TERRORIST.

AL TERRORISMO
LLE MOSCHEE

Where is love?
Where is humanit
STOP THIS VIOLEN
AGAINST LIFE.

FREE SPEECH

In most countries, the media are free to report and comment on events without censorship from the government. With the rise of social media, an unregulated form of media, this freedom can become dangerous. Islamist groups have started to use social media for propaganda and recruitment, but people worry that bringing in regulations might work against other users' freedom.

> Everyone has the right to freedom of opinion and expression; this right includes freedom to hold opinions without interference and to seek, receive and impart information and ideas through any media and regardless of frontiers.

Article 19, The Universal Declaration of Human Rights

PARIS AND *CHARLIE HEBDO*

In January 2015, two gunmen walked into the offices of the *Charlie Hebdo* magazine and murdered twelve of the staff. As they drove away, they killed a police officer. A manhunt followed and two days later, the two men were killed in a shootout with police.

The two men were brothers. They were angered by the magazine printing cartoon images of the Prophet Muhammad (PBUH). The magazine has a long tradition of satirical journalism. It uses humour, exaggeration and ridicule to criticise and comment on world affairs.

Following the attack on the *Charlie Hebdo* offices, many took up the slogan *Je suis Charlie* (I am Charlie) as a show of solidarity for the magazine staff, and a demonstration in support of free speech.

WHO DO TERRORISTS TARGET?

Over time, the type of target that terrorists choose has changed. In the past, they have targeted strategic figures or places that will directly help their cause. Today, their targets also include those with no link to their cause.

A STRATEGIC TARGET

Terrorist targets can relate to a group's overall strategy, as they attack those who are working against them. This might be a military or police base, or a political or military figure.

Boko Haram are an Islamist group active in Nigeria. They are against 'Western education', which includes not only non-religious schooling, but also dress, voting rights and many other ideas they see as coming from a Western influence. They want to overthrow the government and create an Islamist state. They have targeted police and government buildings, the UN headquarters and military barracks.

Places that represent a nation or idea that the terrorist organisation is against can also become targets. In 1998, two US embassies in Dar es Salaam, Tanzania, and Nairobi, Kenya were attacked. It was unclear who was directly behind the attacks, but they were thought to be planned by Osama bin Laden. These are just two of many Islamist attacks against US targets in Africa and the Middle East.

In 2014, 276 schoolgirls were kidnapped by Boko Haram. In 2017, 82 girls were released. Here, Nigerian President, Muhammadu Buhari (rear, centre) sits with their relatives.

THE INNOCENT

The most shocking and upsetting targets for terrorists are the innocent. Attackers have been known to strike locations that are busy, often with people enjoying themselves, such as bars, market places or shopping centres. Terrorists have also been known to target schools, buses and trains where they know that people will be crowded together. In these situations, it is very difficult for people to find shelter and protection.

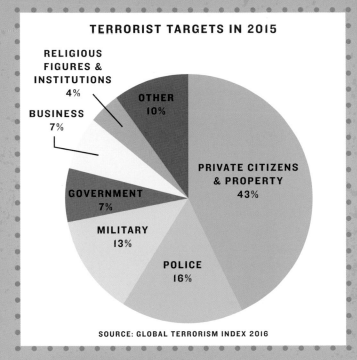

TERRORIST TARGETS IN 2015

- RELIGIOUS FIGURES & INSTITUTIONS 4%
- BUSINESS 7%
- OTHER 10%
- PRIVATE CITIZENS & PROPERTY 43%
- GOVERNMENT 7%
- MILITARY 13%
- POLICE 16%

SOURCE: GLOBAL TERRORISM INDEX 2016

INDIVIDUALS

One of the most horrifying attacks on an individual came in October 2012, when a schoolgirl called Malala Yousafzai was attacked on her way to school. Malala lived in Swat, a region of northern Pakistan ruled by the Taliban. Her father had spoken out against them and their strict religious views. Malala had also spoken against the regime, particularly to stand up for girls' right to education. One day, a gunman stopped her school bus, asked "Who is Malala?" and shot at her. She was injured along with three of her classmates.

In 2013, Malala was chosen as one of *Glamour* magazine's Women of the Year for her work supporting education for girls. Her father (left) went with her to the ceremony.

HOW DO TERRORISTS WORK?

Terrorists often work as opportunists. This means that because they do not have high funds, organised forces or expensive weaponry, they act when they can, using the weapons that are available to them.

BOMBS

An explosive is a substance that can be made to explode, usually by bringing it into contact with high heat. Gunpowder was one of the first explosives to be created and was used in the Gunpowder Plot of 1605 (see page 10). Today, terrorists use explosives to create bombs and other explosive devices. They are able to cause destruction with a relatively small device. Semtex is an explosive that has been used a lot by terrorists because it can be shaped and moulded, and has high explosive power.

Since the 1980s, there has been a rise in the use of suicide bomb attacks. They are used for various reasons: they are difficult to prevent; the devices can be carried by someone with no specialist knowledge or experience; young people can be convinced that this action is honourable; and their shocking nature receives a lot of media attention.

⬇ Trucks fitted with bombs were used to attack synagogues in Istanbul, Turkey, in November 2003. Days later, two more bomb-vehicles were detonated at the British Consulate and the HSBC offices. 53 died and 700 were injured in the four attacks.

HIJACKING

Terrorist strategies that involve hijacking or taking hostages happen less frequently than those using explosives. They take more planning and require more people to work together. Airliners have been targets for hijacking since the late 1940s. When aircraft are hijacked, a large ransom can be demanded for the safe return of the passengers. Vehicles have also been used in recent attacks to deliberately run people over, causing death and severe injuries. Vans were used in attacks on Westminster and Borough, London; and the main city street, Las Ramblas, in Barcelona, Spain in 2017.

PAN AM FLIGHT 103

In December 1988, a plane on route to New York exploded over a town called Lockerbie in Scotland. The 258 people on board died in the explosion, and 11 were killed by falling debris. The blast was caused by a bomb stored in a suitcase. The device had been created from Semtex built into a radio recorder. Most of the passengers were from the USA and it is thought that the organisers were Libyan intelligence agents. It may have been an act of retaliation for the US bombing of Libyan capital Tripoli in 1986.

A garden of rest has been created in Lockerbie, Scotland, to remember the victims of the 1988 attack.

TERROR PLOTS

Between 2013 and 2017, British intelligence services discovered a total of 18 terror plots and were able to stop them. Terrorists often work together to plan, prepare and carry out plots. Small groups working together in this way are known as 'cells'. We know that to prepare for an attack, young Islamists are often sent abroad to training camps before returning to the UK or other countries. It is by watching movements like this that terrorist activity may be detected.

CYBERCRIME

Government services, health and information services and many other businesses and individuals use online systems and data storage on a daily basis. They store vast amounts of information online. Although they are protected, these networks can be attacked in the same way that terrorists attack physical locations. People known as 'hackers' attempt to digitally break into the networks and either steal data or prevent that data from being used.

Many consider the way that terrorists use the internet today as a form of cybercrime. When a terrorist attack occurs, representatives from organisations, such as al-Qaeda, go online to claim responsibility for the attack. They make statements and post further propaganda videos. In 2005, officers from the UK's Scotland Yard arrested a man styling himself as 'Terrorist 007' who had helped to train other terrorists in computer hacking and allowed them to extend their reach in the online world.

RANSOMWARE

In 2017, the UK health services were attacked by something called 'ransomware'. This blocked patient information and demanded money in exchange for lifting the block. Forty regional health services were affected leading to problems treating patients.

When attacked by ransomeware, users will find that their computer screens show a page with a demand for money in exchange for unblocking access to their data and programs.

GLOBAL CYBER ATTACK

In June 2017, computers around the world stopped working and the screen flashed to a ransom note demanding $300 to be paid in the digital currency, bitcoin. Around 2,000 state and public organisations, such as the Ukranian National Bank, were affected, as well as airports, government departments and multi-national companies. With this attack, the 'Petya' ransomware spread quickly between computers.

When this happens, victims are advised not to pay the ransom as there is no guarantee that any of the blocked files will be restored. Instead, people should have all information backed up, so that they can restore the files themselves.

The Maersk shipping and transportation company was just one of the companies hit by the 2017 Petya cyber attack.

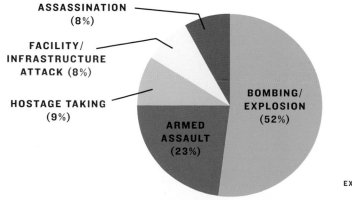

TACTICS USED IN TERRORIST ATTACKS, 2015

ASSASSINATION (8%)

FACILITY/ INFRASTRUCTURE ATTACK (8%)

HOSTAGE TAKING (9%)

ARMED ASSAULT (23%)

BOMBING/ EXPLOSION (52%)

SOURCE: BUREAU OF COUNTERTERRORISM AND COUNTERING VIOLENT EXTREMISM, COUNTRY REPORTS ON TERRORISM 2015.

WHAT IS COUNTER–TERRORISM?

Counter-terrorism is the strategy that governments use to work against terrorism. The strategy in each country may be different, but authorities have similar systems and tools that they can use. To combat terrorism, it is key for countries to work together and to share intelligence.

GOVERNMENT ACTION

One way in which governments tackle terrorism is to fund resources, such as police and intelligence services, so that they can investigate and root out terrorist threats. In addition to this, they can strengthen laws that help to prevent terrorism – such as those that make it a criminal act to finance terrorism. Most recently, governments have been looking at social media regulations and ways that they can remove terrorist content from their platforms.

POLICE

The police work both on the ground and as an intelligence service. You might have seen police officers on the streets, in large public spaces and guarding important buildings. They are there both to watch for any unusual activity and to prevent an attack if it is attempted. After an attack, there is often an increase in armed police presence on the streets. This is both to make people feel safer, and also to try to counter any attacks that might follow from the first one.

MAR 2016 Paris, France, 2016: One of the options after a terrorist attack is for the police or army to have an increased presence on the streets.

INTELLIGENCE

Intelligence services work with the police to investigate possible threats and to find networks of terrorists. This includes monitoring the internet and social media for signs of an attack. The UK security service MI5 reported in 2017 that they were running 500 investigations and looking at 3,000 potential suspects; 81 per cent of their resources go into anti-terrorist investigations.

EARLY INTERVENTION PROGRAMMES

One of the key ways that governments hope to prevent terrorism is to stop radicalisation occurring in the first place. They work with schools and other places of education, healthcare providers, faith groups, places of worship, and charities to try to identify those vulnerable to radicalisation. Once identified, they aim to give these individuals advice and support to prevent them becoming radicalised.

UK GOVERNMENT THREAT LEVELS

Since 2006, the government of the UK have used 'threat levels' to inform the public of the threat from terrorist action. Threat levels range from Low to Critical.

- LOW means an attack is unlikely
- MODERATE means an attack is possible, but not likely
- SUBSTANTIAL means an attack is a strong possibility
- SEVERE means an attack is highly likely
- CRITICAL means an attack is expected imminently

Faith leaders stand together with a victim of the London 2005 attacks, at a conference promoting religious unity in 2015.

WHAT DOES THE FUTURE HOLD?

Although the threat from terrorism today feels immediate and scary, it is important to remember that the threat that each individual faces is low. It is also important to remember that we are surrounded by people who love, help and support us.

COULD TERROR GET WORSE?

Whether terrorism could get worse is impossible to say. However, terrorism is likely to change. As plots are discovered, terrorists will keep trying to re-invent their strategies to remain undiscoverable. As the internet is such a powerful tool in radicalisation and propaganda, it is likely that groups, such as IS, will continue to try to exploit it. Terrorists may also look to change the types of weapons they use. Although use of chemical weapons has not been proved, there is evidence that IS fighters are trained in using them.

Leaving tributes – such as these at at the French Embassy in Ukraine, following the attacks in Paris in 2016 – helps people to show support for the victims' families and friends.

44

HOW DO WE ACHIEVE PEACE?

Many terrorist organisations have risen up over the years. Sometimes military action has been needed to combat them; in other cases, groups have been gradually weakened by policing, and at other times, a political agreement has been reached. Today, policing is more difficult because groups are spread far and wide, and do not need to meet to communicate. Political discussions are limited as many governments refuse to talk to organisations until they stop all violent activity, including terrorism.

With the majority of threats today coming from radical Islamist groups, the strategies for working against them include early intervention to reduce their support, and alliances between those nations who oppose them. The quest for a peaceful solution is ongoing, and is made more difficult by the lack of communication between IS and governments.

A SUCCESSFUL PEACE PROCESS

The Good Friday Agreement signed in 1998 marked the end of the 'Troubles' in Northern Ireland (see page 15). Although there have been incidents since, peace has largely held. The agreement created a power–sharing government in Northern Ireland that made sure no one party could dominate decision making. Certain powers were also transferred to the Northern Ireland government from the UK government in Westminster, London.

This is one example of a peaceful political resolution to a violent struggle.

Stormont Palace, Belfast, is the seat of the Northern Ireland power-sharing government, established by the peace process.

GLOSSARY

ASSASSINATION – killing someone for political or religious reasons

CEASEFIRE – when fighting is temporarily suspended, by one or both sides

CENSORSHIP – control of content that appears in news, books, films or other forms of media

CONFISCATION – taking something that belongs to someone else

DETONATE – set off an explosive device

DISSIDENT – someone who is against the official policy of the state

ESCALATION – an increase or worsening

ETHNICITY – belonging to a social group where people have the same cultural traditions

EXPLOIT – to use for your own gain or benefit

FOLK RELIGIONS – faiths that originate from a group of people, ethnicity or tribe. Examples include African traditional religions, Chinese folk religions, Native American religions and Australian aboriginal religions.

HADITH – the sayings of the Prophet Muhammad (PBUH) and his companions

INSURGENT – a group that work against those in power

INTIMIDATE – to frighten someone into doing what you want them to

ISLAMIST – someone who practices a fundamental or extreme form of Islam, and supports violence

MILITANT – a person or group that support violent ways of supporting a political cause

NARCO-TERRORISM – terrorism that is funded by illegal drug trade, and violence associated with this trade; 'narco' comes from the word 'narcotics' which is another word for drugs

PROPAGANDA – information that is biased or misleading, that supports a belief or cause

PROPHET – a person on earth who is believed to be able to communicate with a god, and therefore bring the god's message to ordinary people

REGIME – a system of government

SABOTAGE – to damage or destroy something to hold back enemy forces or activities

SECT – a small group with different beliefs to those of the larger group they belong to

SUPREMACIST – someone who believes that one group is superior to another, usually on grounds of race

TAMIL – someone who belongs to a cultural group who live in South India and Sri Lanka

TORTURE – using pain to try to get information from someone

TRAFFICKING – trading in something illegal, for example, drug trafficking

VULNERABLE – describes someone who is at risk of being harmed or attacked

FURTHER INFORMATION

BOOKS

Following a Faith series (*A Jewish Life, A Hindu Life, A Muslim Life, A Christian Life*),
Cath Senker, Franklin Watts, 2017/2018

I am Malala, Malala Yousafzai with Christina Lamb, Phoenix, 2014

Terrorism (Global Issues), Alex Woolf, Wayland, 2014

Towers Falling, Jewell Parker Rhodes, Little Brown Young Readers, 2017 (Fiction)

Uprisings in the Middle East (Behind the News), Philip Steele, Wayland, 2014

Who are Refugees and Migrants? What Makes People Leave their Homes? And Other Big Questions,
Michael Rosen and Annemarie Young, Wayland, 2016

Why Do We Fight?: Conflict, War and Peace, Niki Walker, Franklin Watts, 2014

WEBSITES

Find advice if you are upset by what you see on the news:
www.bbc.co.uk/newsround/13865002

Find information and advice on Childline's 'Worries about the world' page:
www.childline.org.uk/info-advice/your-feelings/anxiety-stress-panic/worries-about-the-world

Learn more about different world religions:
www.bbc.co.uk/religion

A BBC guide to what radicalisation is and why people join IS:
www.bbc.co.uk/newsround/33599779

The UK government's page of advice for the public in the event of an attack:
www.gov.uk/government/publications/stay-safe-film

INDEX